# My First Hundred Words
# I Need

# My First Hundred Words I Need to Know!

Roz Brookz

Published by **talkwell2writewell.co.uk** ©

# What can I learn with the 1 and 2 letter words?

## grammar & punctuation

I can speak or write these words in interesting sentences.

## puzzles & games

I can play "Snap!"

"Match-the-Pairs"

"Find-a-Rhyme"

## reading & writing

I can trace, colour, copy, read and spell the words.

I can make sentences and stories with the words and pictures.

## phonics & spelling

I can learn the sound, name and shape of each letter and letter blend.

I can chop and change the letters to make new words.

## speaking & listening

I can find other words with 1 or 2 letters.

I can use my words for let's pretend, storytelling, imagining.

# What can I do with all the 1 and 2 letter words?

colour cut stick

chop change copy trace

add them to

**My Story Teller's Dictionary**

imagine pretend

make believe

tell tall tales

chat rap listen gossip

talk play

# Penguin's challenge choice.

On the pages of Multi-sensory

**-activities** with **1 & 2** letter words-

**-activities** with **3 & 4** letter words-

**-activities** with **5 & more** letter words-

...can you use the pictures and some of the words to make sentences, stories or poems?

Can you choose some words,
cut them out and lay them on a flat surface?
Can you think of exciting words
to fill the gaps between these words?

## Now you can to create wonderful tales to tell your friends and family!

# IDEA!

Print pages 55 to 66
Laminate each page.
Cut out the words.

Use sticky tack which may
or may not be blue,
and display on a tea tray,
baking tray, clip board or similar.

Use them to spell check.

Choose from your 100 words to plan
and scaffold your story making.

Use

## My Story Teller's Dictionary

to store and refer to
all the one hundred words.

**It is very clear these resources have been created by someone who understands how children learn. Highly recommended.**
**~ S. Ashley -reception class teacher Cornwall Education**

# Before You Start!

Don't want to cut up your
beautiful new book?
These pages can purchased to
download as PDFs.
Print any size and
as many as your child needs.

Just go to our web site

https://talkwell2writewell.co.uk/

Download these beautifully produced,
lessons for your child to
cut up, copy, learn
and enjoy using again and again.

Add the **First Hundred Words** to
**My Story Teller's Dictionary**
Available in paperback at Amazon.co.uk
and to download and print at

https://talkwell2writewell.co.uk/

# Before You Start!

## Photocopying your paperback book.

Permission is given to make copies for use within your family /household

## What weight paper shall I use?

**80-120 GSM**-use for single use, practice sheets and cutting and sticking pages. Most often used office paper.

**130-250 GSM**-use for pages you want to keep, add to and refer to. E.g. posters, book covers, research projects, to keep and display, and for…

**My Story Teller's Dictionary**

**My 1st 100 Words I Need to Know!**

**260-300 GSM**- Thick but still bendable, use for posters, book covers, research projects, to keep and display.

**Not all pages need to be copied.**

# Before You Start!

**You will need to copy these pages...**

**on single sheets for cutting and sticking into**
**My Story Teller's Dictionary**

## Pages 2 10-20

1 and 2 letter words I can add to
**My Story Teller's Dictionary**

## Pages 24-33 35-44

3 and 4 letter words I can add to
**My Story Teller's Dictionary**

## Pages 48-53

5 and more letter words I can add to
**My Story Teller's Dictionary**

## Pages 55-66

100 words I can **copy or stick into**
**My Story Teller's Dictionary**

## Pages 70-94

100 words I can
**learn to read, write and spell**

_____________'s

# book of

# My 1st 100 Words I Need to Know

Talk Well 2 Write Well

# One and two letter words I can add to

# My Story Teller's Dictionary

Talk Well 2 Write Well

You can cut out and stick into

My Story Teller's Dictionary.

Or you can use your best

hand writing to copy the words.

Have a go at reading and spelling them.

| | |
|---|---|
| a | as |
| he | I |
| an | be |
| me | at |

# Multi-sensory **activities** with **1 & 2** letter words.

Penguin's Challenge by Choice…can you…

…use these pictures and some of the one and two letter words to make sentences, stories or poems?

For example…….

A robin sat on a branch and sang
As hard as he could,
His sweet song rang,
He gave his best tweet
Then flew down the street
And landed, so proudly,
On the top of a tree.

But the Jester,
he boasted,
"Just look at me!
I am so high,so much
higher than thee.
My statue is tall,
As tall as can be."

The robin looked up
with a gleam in his eye,
"That may be so,
But you can't fly!"

Poem by Roz tw2ww©

a
as
he
I
an
be
me
at

Multi-sensory **activities** with **1 & 2** letter words.

**Keep working your voice, eyes and hands to help your brain achieve automatic recall.**

Then you can say:

"I can read and spell the most often used one and two letter words!"

| | |
|---|---|
| o r | i n |
| n o | o f |
| o n | s o |
| m y | d o |

Multi-sensory **activities** with **1 & 2** letter words.

Penguin's Challenge by Choice…can you…

…use these pictures and some of the one and two letter words to make sentences, stories or poems?

example

The Chinook

can land on the ground or on an aircraft carrier but it cannot land in the sea.

The balloon flies so far, yet it has no engine.

There are no blue planes in my favourite

flying team,

The Red Arrows.

or
in
no
of
on
so
my
do

## More words for

# My Story Teller's Dictionary

It's important to keep using your words so your voice, ears, eyes and hands can train your brain to remember them.

| | |
|---|---|
| b y | t o |
| w e | i f |
| u p | u s |
| i t | g o |

Multi-sensory **activities** with **1 & 2** letter words.

Penguin's Challenge by Choice…can you…

…use these pictures and some of the one and two letter words to make sentences, stories or poems?

example

Kay holds Penguin gently up to the glass.

If she bangs the glass it will alarm the real penguin and it will go away.

We will be sad if she does that.

up
to
we
if
by
go
it
us

Penguin's Challenge by Choice:
Can you use your best handwriting to add more two letter words

from the list below?

Choose four to copy into the yellow block, then cut them out and stick them into

**My Story Teller's Dictionary**

example

ah am

aw

uh um

ha hi

pi ye

yo

# What can I do with all the three and four letter words?

colour cut stick

chop change copy trace

add them to

**My Story Teller's Dictionary**

imagine pretend

make believe

tell tall tales

chat rap listen gossip

talk play

# What can I learn with the three and four letter words?

### grammar & punctuation

I can speak or write these words in interesting sentences.

### puzzles & games

I can play "Snap!"

"Match-the-Pairs"

"Find-a-Rhyme"

### reading & writing

I can trace, colour, copy, read and spell the words.

I can make sentences and stories with the words and pictures.

### phonics & spelling

I can learn the sound, name and shape of each letter and letter blend.

I can chop and change the letters to make new words.

### speaking & listening

I can find other words with 3 or 4 letters.

I can use my words for let's pretend, storytelling, imagining.

# Three and four letter words I can add to

# My Story Teller's Dictionary

talkwell2writewell.co.uk

Multi-sensory **activities** with **3 & 4** letter words.

Cut out and stick into

## My Story Teller's Dictionary

Use your best hand writing to copy the words.

Have a go at reading and spelling them.

| | |
|---|---|
| s h e | t w o |
| w h o | y o u |
| t h e | u s e |
| n o t | b u t |
| t h i s | w a y |

Penguin's Challenge by Choice...can you...

...use the pictures and any of the three and four letter words to make up

sentences, stories or poems?

example

The man climbs the tower but he becomes stuck.

**Supernurse** will use his super powers and this will save him.

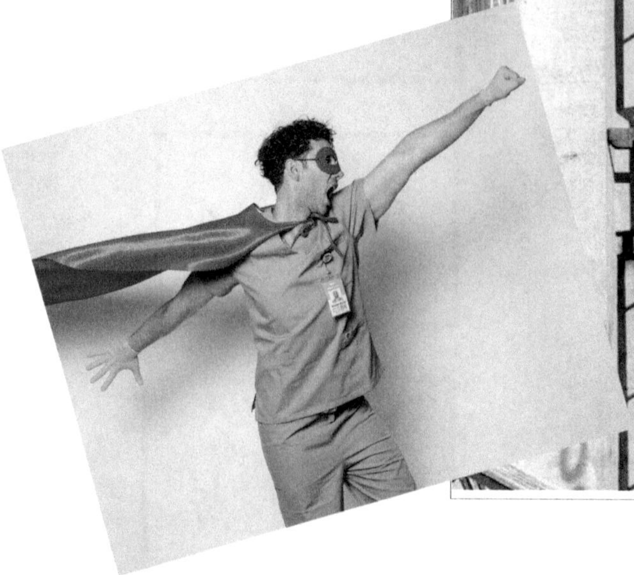

Multi-sensory **activities** with **3 & 4** letter words.

Keep that learning brain working.

Play games of Snap! or "Find-a-Rhyme."

Colour, illustrate, display your work.

# Multi-sensory **activities** with **3 & 4** letter words.

## More words for

## My Story Teller's Dictionary

It's important to keep using your words so your voice, ears, eyes and hands can train your brain to remember them.

| | |
|---|---|
| h i s | s a y |
| o u t | w i l l |
| o n e | g e t |
| s e e | n o w |
| o u r | n e w |

## Multi-sensory **activities** with **3 & 4** letter words.

Penguin's Challenge by Choice…can you…

…use the pictures and any of the three and four letter words to make up sentences, stories or poems?

example

We see our rescue helicopter arrive. It is a new one.

The crew member has his survival suit on and is now out of the aircraft.

He will get down to the water and one by one, he will winch us to safety.

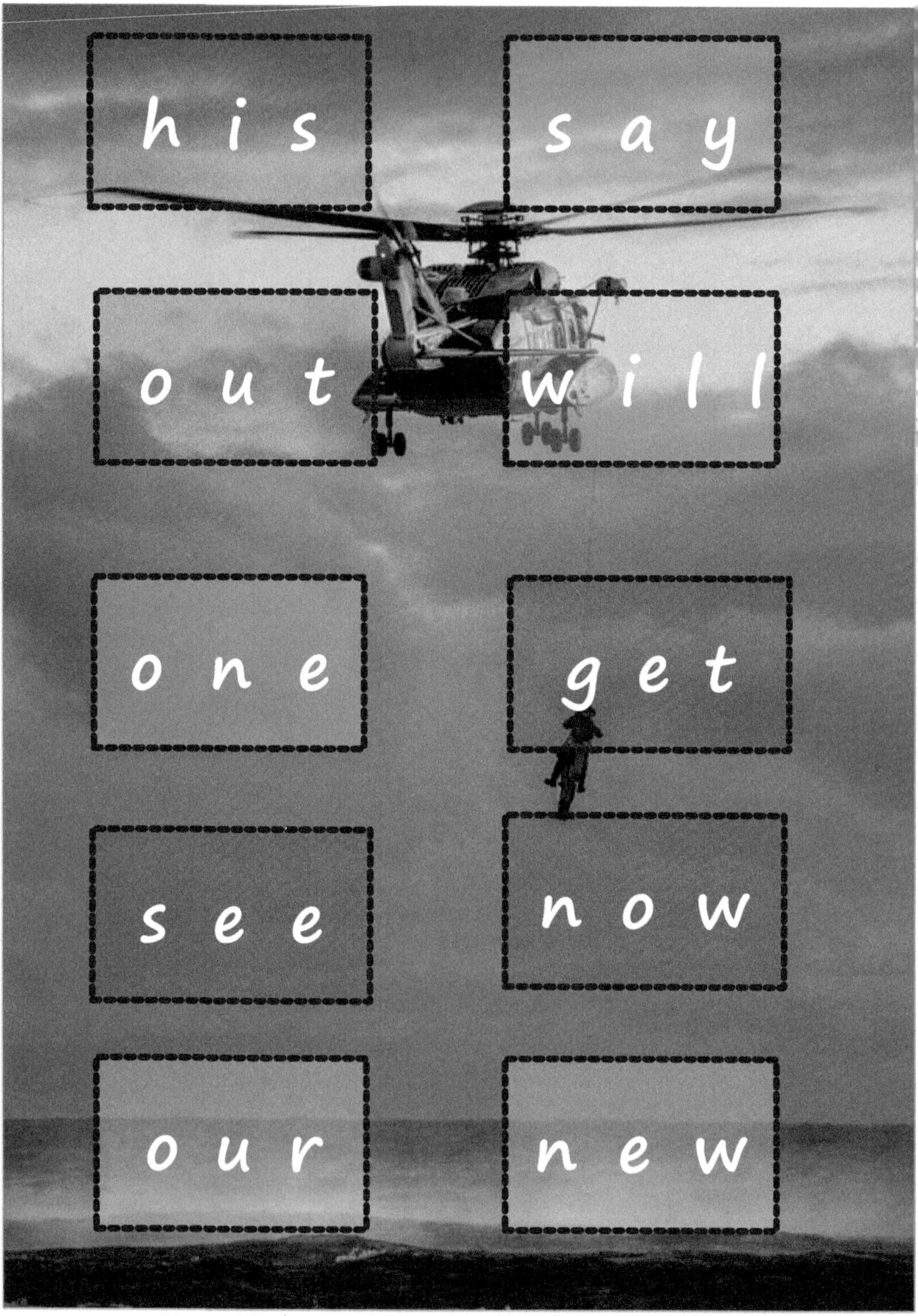
h i s
s a y
o u t
w i l l
o n e
g e t
s e e
n o w
o u r
n e w

Multi-sensory **activities** with **3 & 4** letter words.

More words for

# My Story Teller's Dictionary.

It's important to keep using your words so your voice, ears, eyes and hands can train your brain to remember them.

| | |
|---|---|
| c a n | a n y |
| d a y | a n d |
| a l l | h e r |
| f o r | h i m |
| h o w | i t s |

Penguin's Challenge by Choice…can you…

…use the pictures and any of the three and four letter words to make up

sentences, stories or poems?

example

Sam can wear his red shirt all day as it keeps him cool.

The van carries its cargo of gnomes. The driver likes the gnome with the lantern and drops him at Sam's house.

The gnome would like a lady gnome friend, so he can keep her safe at night, with his lantern.

c a n
a n y
d a y
a n d

a l l
h e r
f o r
h i m
h o w
i t s

Penguin's Parent Challenge...

Can you be the teacher and test your brothers and sisters, Mums and Dads, grandparents? Can they find a word to rhyme with any of these?

| | |
|---|---|
| also | give |
| back | good |
| come | have |
| even | into |
| from | just |

## Multi-sensory **activities** with **3 & 4** letter words.

Penguin's Challenge by Choice…can you…

…use these pictures and some of the three and four letter words to make sentences, stories or poems?

Can you cut out the words, lay them out and use exciting words to fill the gaps between them.

Now you can to create wonderful tales

to tell your friends and family?

example

My brother is a good cook and I am also good at it.

We have fun just being with Gran and Pappy, even if we do have to clean up afterwards.

We give some cakes to Mum and Dad, and they always come back for more.

also
give
back
good
come
have
even
into
from
just

Multi-sensory **activities** with **3 & 4** letter words.

Keeping working your voice, ears, eyes and hands to elp your brain achieve automatic recall. Then you can ay:

'I can read and spell the first one hundred words!

| | |
|---|---|
| know | only |
| like | over |
| look | some |
| make | take |
| most | than |

Penguin's Challenge by Choice…can you…

…use these pictures and some of the

Three and four letter words to make sentences, stories or poems?

example

My dog, Petra, took one look at the sausages and tiptoed over to take some.

Mum and Gran did not know Petra would like some sausages and only found out when they saw she had eaten most of them.

They will have to make some more!

This is a true story!

know
only
like
over
look
some
make
take
most
than

Multi-sensory **activities** with **3 & 4** letter words. There are lots **th** words here, and two **wh** words, so don't just see the first two letters, then guess the rest! **Look, cover, write** and **check** the whole word!

| | |
|---|---|
| that | time |
| them | want |
| then | well |
| they | what |
| | when |

Penguin's Challenge by Choice…can you…

..use these pictures and some of the Three and four letter words to make sentences, stories or poems?

example

The excavator drivers work very well to complete the railway on time. They want to be sure that the trains can run safely.

Then the trains can run and they can carry passengers, who love what they see on this journey.

that
time
them
want
NEW HOLLAND
then
well
they
what
when

Multi-sensory **activities** with **3 & 4** letter words.

Keep using your best handwriting and grow those neural pathways in your brain!

and make sure you

spell it right or you will learn it wrong!

(Please excuse the grammar here!)

with

work

year

your

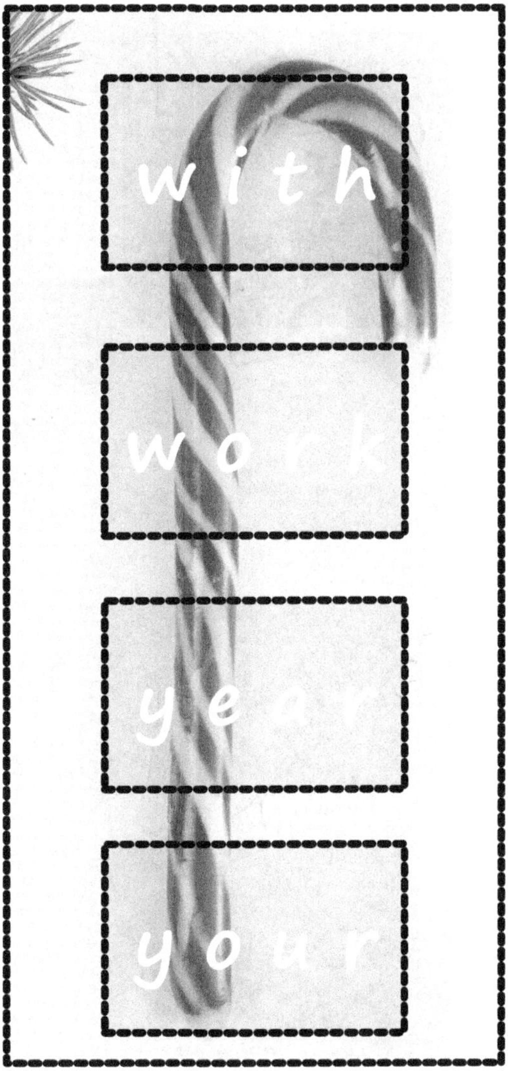

Penguin's Challenge by Choice…can you…

…use these pictures and some of the

Three and four letter words to make sentences, stories or poems?

example

You can't hear for a year,

With cake in your ear!

You can't work for a year,

With that cake in your ear!

Your Mama said, "Work,"

But before next year

She came with your Papa

To give you a cheer.

Penguin's Challenge by Choice:

Can you use your best handwriting to add more three and four letter words?

Use the blocks below to write your words , then cut them out and stick them into

| | |
|---|---|
| example<br>hand<br>pig | |

# What can I do with all the five and more letter words?

colour cut stick

chop change copy trace

add them to

**My Story Teller's Dictionary**

imagine pretend

make believe

tell tall tales

chat rap listen gossip

talk play

# What can I learn with the five and more letter words?

### grammar & punctuation

I can speak or write these words in interesting sentences.

### puzzles & games

I can play "Snap!"

"Match-the-Pairs"

"Find-a-Rhyme"

### reading & writing

I can trace, colour, copy, read and spell the words.

I can make sentences and stories with the words and pictures.

### phonics & spelling

I can learn the sound, name and shape of each letter and letter blend.

I can chop and change the letters to make new words.

### speaking & listening

I can find other words with 5 or more letters.

I can use my words for pretending, storytelling, imagining.

# Five and more letter words I can add to

# My Story Teller's Dictionary

Talk Well 2 Write Well

talkwell2writewell.co.uk

Keep working your voice, ears, eyes and hands to help your brain achieve automatic recall. Then you can say:

"I can read and spell the first one hundred words!"

a b o u t

f i r s t

a f t e r

o t h e r

b e c a u s e

p e r s o n

Penguin's Challenge by Choice...can you...
...use the pictures and any of the
Five and more letter words to make up
sentences, stories or poems?

example

The boy is about to go on the rope swing, but because the other boy gets there first, he has to wait until after that boy has jumped off.

a b o u t
f i r s t
a f t e r
o t h e r
b e c a u s e
p e r s o n

# Multi-sensory **activities** with 5++ letter words.

Keep working your voice, ears, eyes and hands to help your brain achieve automatic recall.

Then you can say:

"I can read and spell the first one hundred words!"

w o u l d

t h e i r

t h e s e

t h e r e

t h i n k

c o u l d

w h i c h

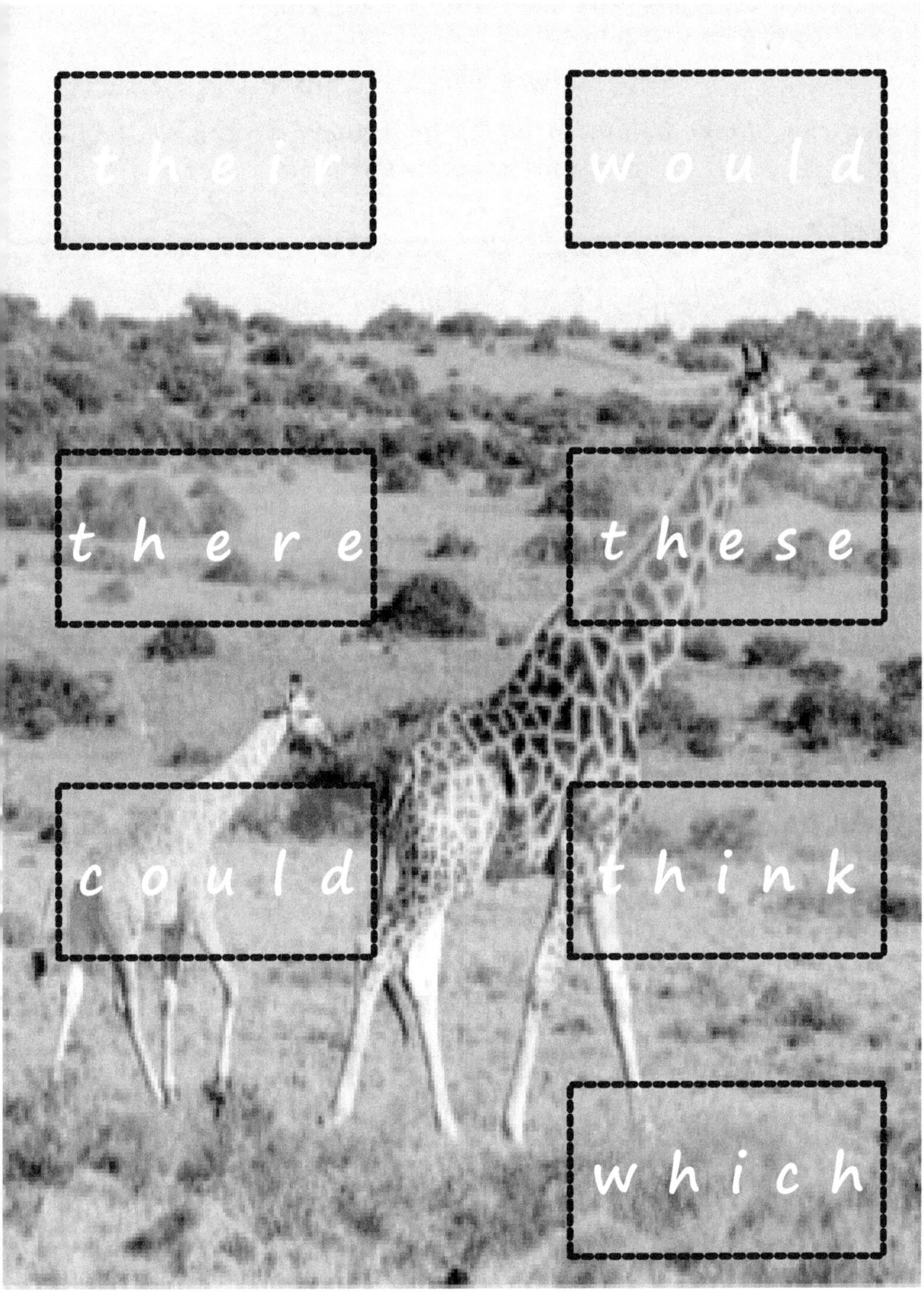
t h e i r
w o u l d
t h e r e
t h e s e
c o u l d
t h i n k
w h i c h

Penguin's Challenge by Choice:
Can you use your best handwriting to add extra five or more letter words?

Use the blocks below to write your words , then cut them out and stick them into

My Story Teller's Dictionary

One Hundred
words I can
copy or stick
into
My Story Teller's
Dictionary
Talk Well 2 Write Well
talkwell2writewell.co.uk

# A hundred words to add to My Story Teller's Dictionary

Cut out and stick into

**My Story Teller's Dictionary**

Use your best hand writing to copy the words.
Have a go at reading, writing and spelling them

| | |
|---|---|
| a | as |
| he | I |
| an | be |
| me | at |

# A hundred words to add to My Story Teller's Dictionary

**Keep working your voice, ears, eyes and hands to help your brain achieve automatic recall.**

Then you can say:

"I can read and spell the most often used one and two letter words!"

| | |
|---|---|
| o r | i n |
| n o | o f |
| o n | s o |
| m y | d o |

# A hundred words to add to My Story Teller's Dictionary

More words for My Story Teller's Dictionary.

It's important to keep using your words so your voice, ears, eyes and hands can train your brain to remember them.

| | |
|---|---|
| by | to |
| we | if |
| up | us |
| it | go |

# A hundred words to add to My Story Teller's Dictionary

Cut out and stick into

My Story Teller's Dictionary.

Use your best hand writing to copy the words.

Have a go at reading, spelling and writing them.

| | |
|---|---|
| s h e | t w o |
| w h o | y o u |
| t h e | u s e |
| n o t | b u t |
| t h i s | w a y |

# A hundred words to add to My Story Teller's Dictionary

More words for My Story Teller's Dictionary.

It's important to keep using your words so your voice, ears, eyes and hands can

train your brain to remember them.

| | |
|---|---|
| h i s | s a y |
| o u t | w i l l |
| o n e | g e t |
| s e e | n o w |
| o u r | n e w |

# A hundred words to add to My Story Teller's Dictionary

More words for My Story Teller's Dictionary.

It's important to keep using your words so your voice, ears, eyes and hands can

train your brain to remember them.

| | |
|---|---|
| can | any |
| day | and |
| all | her |
| for | him |
| how | its |

# A hundred words to add to My Story Teller's Dictionary

Penguin's Parent Challenge...

You be the teacher...test your brothers and sisters, Mums and Dads, grandparents...

Can they find a word to rhyme with any of these?

| | |
|---|---|
| also | give |
| back | good |
| come | have |
| even | into |
| from | just |

# A hundred words to add to My Story Teller's Dictionary

Keeping working your voice, ears, eyes and hands to help your brain achieve automatic recall. Then you can say:

"I can read and spell the first one hundred words!"

| | |
|---|---|
| know | only |
| like | over |
| look | some |
| make | take |
| most | than |

# A hundred words to add to My Story Teller's Dictionary

There are lots **th** words here, and two **wh** words, so don't just see the first two letters, then guess the rest!

**Look, cover, write** and **check** the whole word!

that

them

then

they

time

want

well

what

when

# A hundred words to add to My Story Teller's Dictionary

Keep using your best handwriting and grow those neural pathways in your brain!

**and make sure you**

**spell it right or you will learn it wrong!**

(Please excuse the grammar here!)

with

work

year

your

# A hundred words to add to My Story Teller's Dictionary

Keep working your voice, ears, eyes and hands to help your brain achieve automatic recall. Then you can say:

"I can read and spell the first one hundred words!"

a b o u t

f i r s t

a f t e r

o t h e r

b e c a u s e

p e r s o n

# A hundred words to add to My Story Teller's Dictionary

**Keep working your voice, ears, eyes and hands to help your brain achieve automatic recall.** Then you can say:

"I can read and spell the

first one hundred words!"

| | |
|---|---|
| | w o u l d |
| t h e i r | t h e s e |
| t h e r e | t h i n k |
| c o u l d | w h i c h |

# One hundred words
# I can read, write and spell

Penguin's challenge by choice, can you...

...use the following pages
and learn to read, spell and write your First Hundred Words?

Can you...

...colour or trace the words? 

...cut out and stuck some into

My Story Teller's Dictionary?

...draw pictures and make posters with the words?

Penguin says, you don't have to do this all immediately.

You can use a few words at a time, and gradually build your dictionary.

You can choose some to make a story or poem.

You can illustrate your creative writing.

You can learn your
First Hundred Words
as and when
you need them.

One hundred words
I can
read, write
and spell
Talk Well 2 Write Well
talkwell2writewell.co.uk

# One hundred words I can read, write and spell

You can use the hundred words in any of these ways.

Give it a go!

chop

change

copy

trace

read

write

spell

punctuate

colour

cut

stick

chat

listen

sign

gossip

talk

play

imagine

pretend

make believe

rhyme

rap

sing

puppets

drama

# One hundred words
# I can read, write and spell

a as at an

a as at an

a as at an

a as at an

a as at an

a as at an

I I I I I I I I

me me me me

he he he he he

be be be be be

One hundred words
I can read, write and spell

on on on on on

in in in in in

of of of of of of

or or or or or

so so so so so

my my my my

do do do do do

no no no no no

# One hundred words
# I can read, write and spell

by by by by by

to to to to to

we we we we

if if if if if

# One hundred words
# I can read, write and spell

up up up up

us us us us us

go go go go

it it it it it it

# One hundred words
# I can read, write and spell

she she she she

too too too too

you you you

who who who

One hundred words

I can read, write and spell

the use not but

the use not but

the use not but

the use not but

this this this

way way way

say say say

out out out

# One hundred words
# I can read, write and spell

his his his his

will will will will

get get get get

one one one one

# One hundred words
## I can read, write and spell

see see see see

our our our our

now now now

new new new

# One hundred words
# I can read, write and spell

can can can can

any any any any

day day day day

and and and

# One hundred words
# I can read, write and spell

all all all all

her her her

for for for for

him him him

how how how

its its its

give give give

also also also

# One hundred words
# I can read, write and spell

back back back

good good good

come come

have have have

# One hundred words
## I can read, write and spell

even even even

into into into

just just just

from from

# One hundred words
# I can read, write and spell

know know

only only only

like like like

over over over

look look

some some

make make

take take

## One hundred words
## I can read, write and spell

most than want time

most than want time

# One hundred words
# I can read, write and spell

them

then

they

that

them

then

they

that

# One hundred words
# I can read, write and spell

well what when with

well what when with

work

year

your

about

work

year

your

about

after

other

person

first

after

other

person

first

# One hundred words
# I can read, write and spell

because

would

could

which

because

would

could

which

these

think

there

their

these

think

there

their

# Meet the team!

Hi, I am Roz. I've been a teacher and in education, including a schools inspector, for my entire working life. Now retired, I have started a company called

talk well 2 write well... why?

Let me explain.

I started my career as a young teacher, teaching English, reading, writing, and spelling, all that good stuff. It all went well, except there was one major problem that kept coming up.

A lot of the pupils couldn't spell and just kept having so much difficulty learning to read and write fluently. It was heart breaking to see them struggling and failing.

These pupils weren't lazy or naughty. They were lovely, everyday children who were struggling with learning how to read and write. So we sat down and figured out what was going wrong and how we could get them learning; now I could get them back on track, but what about next year?

Now, this happened year after year until I had had enough. I needed to find out why these pupils were struggling and what could be done about it. I looked up all the research I could find and put it into place in my classroom, over the years, turning my research into a system that worked.

Not wanting to keep it secret, I decided to show the world the system I had developed through years of trial and error and show parents how they can help and teach their children, and this is what tw2ww has become.

Talk well 2 write well is a series that will show you how to teach your child to imagine their first stories, tell their first tales , read and write their first sentences and beyond.

Because, in my experience, before children can write well, they must talk well.

I have always found that the time-tested and well-researched teaching method of multi-sensory learning greatly improves reading and writing.

That's how I delivered the classes over all my years in education.

I am a teacher with over 40 years of experience teaching pupils and students from 4 to 64 years old. I was a class teacher, a program manager for disengaged teenagers, head of foundation studies at an FE College, a Registered Ofsted Inspector for Nurseries and lead practitioner for the Cornwall Virtual School, which oversees the education of children in care, both in and out of school. I still enjoy teaching online across a wide range of abilities.

I have been joined at talkwell2writewell, by my son Christian, to make a family business. I write the education content, and he does the marketing and Internet stuff.

We are a good team, working mainly remotely between Cornwall and Worcestershire, and we would love for you and your child to join us as we change the game in online teaching.

I wish you all the best in teaching your children.

**Rosalind Brooks. Hon BA Education**

PS. Christian says Hi, and he would love to get to know you; he hangs out on Facebook; just search Talkwell2writewell.

PS...PS. If you want to try us for free, have a book on us.

**Christian Ayerst. BSc Psychology**

Find us at https://talkwell2writewell.co.uk

# More from talkwell2writewell...

At www.talkwell2writewell.co.uk
we are committed to teaching NOT testing.

Our books offer English language based activities.
Every page is designed to engage and reward your child's efforts, with fabulous photographs to excite their imagination, plus child friendly fonts and layouts,
encouraging enjoyment and
the wish to work.

We offer books at three stages

- Pika Stage Ages 5 to 7 years, or thereabouts
- Panda Stage Ages 7 to 9 years, or thereabouts
- Panther Stage Ages 9 to 11 years, or thereabouts

Your child is kept busy working off screen with words and pictures to move, match and sort, chop and change. Fundamental to our vision are speaking and listening, or sign language, because we must all talk well to write well!
Your child is supported to
create, tell, write and read their stories.
Multi-sensory skills are seamlessly interwoven
with language development.

**COMING SOON!**

to our **TIWIK** pages for your

child's individual record of achievement

ALL YOUR National Curriculum targets for English

This Is What I Know. Y1 Y2 Y3 Y4 Y5 & Y6

All our books are perfect as reference texts to
plan lessons, set targets and check progress.
They are available in either paperback from Amazon.co.uk
or to download from our web site,
so you can print them in a size to suit your child.
**PLUS, with every book you can**
**make multiple copies to use within your household.**

Introducing research skills from an early age, enables your child to find and read information and, in their own words, record their findings, in projects, posters, presentations.
We don't do "Google-copy-paste-I'm done!"

# FREE STUFF!

# Get Your Freebies HERE!

All these can be downloaded
FOR FREE from our website.

Find us at https://talkwell2writewell.co.uk

## Story Frames and Planners
in
Pika, Panda and Panther Stages
5 to 11 year olds

## FREE spelling Lists
in
Pika, Panda and Panther Stages
5 to 11 year olds

ALL word lists are from the
UK National Curriculum for English
KS1 and KS2
PLUS many additional
linked words and spellings

Published by **talkwell2writewell.co.uk**

Printed in Great Britain
by Amazon

24006430R10056